Here's what peop
Jannah Jewels ⸗

I can't continue without sayi
Muslim Girls! No damsels in di
no cliché girly nonsense! ... Thi
up reading.
–Emma Apple, Author of best-selling 'Children's First Questions'
Islamic Book Series

The Jannah Jewels books are awesome. They have made my daughters
love to read with characters that dress like them and names they are
familiar with. The stories keep their attention and make them curious
about times past and present. We love Jannah Jewels at our house.
-Jessica Colon

The Jannah Jewels series are exactly what I would write if I had the
gift of creative writing! As a mother, they are fun to read aloud as
well as for the child to get immersed in! This series is the perfect blend
of history, mystery, adventure and Islam! My daughter has even
recommended these to her non-Muslim friends and was inspired
to do a 'show and tell' on Mansa Musa thanks to these books! I'm
thankful for these engaging stories and the strong female characters,
thank you to the authors for a job well done, we can't wait for the rest
of the series!
-Nazia Ullah

I like how you combine adventure and Islamic concepts to make us
readers want to know more and more about the series. I am addicted
to Jannah Jewels and I can't wait to find when and how they will get
the artifact in America!
-Subhana Saad, Age 8

Fantastic book! My child was turning pages and couldn't wait to read
the next chapter. So much so he's asking for the next book in the series.
-Mrs. S. A. Khanom, Book Reviewer

We loved the Jannah Jewels books! There are very few Muslim books for kids that are entertaining. The Jannah Jewels books were very fun to read. They were so good that we read the entire series in two days!
-Zayd & Sofia Tayeb, age 10 & 7

I could really feel the love that went into this book – the characters, the places, the history, and the things that the author clearly strongly believes in and wants to share with our children and the wider world through her heroines…My daughter's verdict? "I would give the book a 10 out of 10 mum"
–Umm Salihah, HappyMuslimah.com Blog

I have a 9 year old boy and 5 year old girl. Both are very good readers now only because of Jannah Jewels. There are times when they were addicted to the screen. But Jannah Jewels changed everything upside down. The interesting characters, way of narration, adventure, artwork and messages make it more real in my kids' world and help them take the morals to heart. It changed their behavior a lot and made them good kids.
-Shaniya Arafath

My 8 year old loves this series - so much so that she has told all her friends about it, and one of them even gifted a couple more Jannah Jewels books for her birthday! In fact, I found myself reading her books much to the delight of my daughter - and then we both discussed our favorite parts. I love how the writers combine Islamic history with fun story lines and cute picture depictions. My daughter loves to sketch - and her books are filled with the Jannah Jewels character drawings. I would buy this series again and again. Thank you for all your wonderful work!
-Ruku Kazia

Learning about Islamic history and famous Muslims of the past makes these books a historical book lover's wish, and the Islamic twist is a plus for young Muslim readers. Jannah Jewels has been Muslimommy approved as kid-friendly!
-Zakiyya Osman, MusliMommy.com

I love all of the Jannah Jewels books, and the fact that you combine history and adventure in your stories. I also liked that you put the holy verses of Quran that remind us to stay close to Allah and I liked the fact that in one book you mentioned the verse from Quran which mentions the benefit of being kind to your enemy. I have read all of the Jannah Jewels books and even read two of these books in one day, that's how much I like these books!
–Fatima Bint Saifurrehman, Age 8

My kids liked the characters because they are modest in their mannerisms and dress, so that was something my daughter could relate to. Even though the characters are girls, it had enough excitement and the presence of supporting male characters to be read by both girls and boys. Throughout the book there was an essence of Islamic values and there was a lot of adventure to keep us guessing!
-HomeStudyMama, Book Reviewer

Jannah jewels are the best islamic adventure books I have ever read! The characters are each unique with their own special talents. My uncle bought me the first two books for my 9th birthday and I loved the books straight away. And even asked him to buy the other books too. I love how their hijabs have different styles and I want to become an archer like Hidayah!
-Jannah Yasmeen, Age 9

It's important for girls and boys, Muslim and not, to have strong, non-stereotyped female role models. Jannah jewels bring that in a unique way with a twist on time travel, fantasy, super heroes and factual Muslim history. It is beautifully written, engaging and an absolute must for any Muslim (and non-Muslim) kids library! My daughter LOVES The Jannah Jewels…
–Hani, Book Reviewer

We've reviewed 100s of Islamic non-fiction and fiction books from every single continent, except Antarctica, and none of the fiction books have made such an impression on our family as Jannah Jewels.
–Ponn M. Sabra, Best-selling author, AmericanMuslimMom.com

By Tayyaba Syed & Umm Nura

Vancouver

A very special thank you to S. Imady for giving us the opportunity to use her song lyrics from her forthcoming book, "There's A Love."

To my spiritual family: thank you for your countless breezes of sweet supplications that lights up my path. You are my 'golden' companions and I am so grateful for you. –U.N.

To my beloved siblings Aisha, Ahad, Haleema and their beautiful families: your sincere love and support shines the way for me every single day. I can't thank each of you enough. –T.S.

Published by Gentle Breeze Books, Vancouver, B.C., Canada

Copyright 2016 by Umm Nura
Illustrations by Clarice Menguito

Visit us on the Web! www.JannahJewels.com

ISBN:978-1-988337-02-9
November 2016

Contents

Sport:

Archery

Role:

Guides and leads the girls

Superpower:

Intense sight and spiritual insight

Fear:

Spiders

Special Gadget:

Ancient Compass

Carries:

Bow and Arrow, Ancient Map, Compass

HIDAYAH

Sport:

Skateboarding

Role:

Artist, Racer

Superpower:

Fast racer on foot or skateboard

Fear:

Hunger (She's always hungry!)

Special Gadget:

Time Travel Watch

Carries:

Skateboard, Sketchpad, Pencil, Watch

JAIDE

Sport:

Horseback Riding

Role:

Walking Encyclopedia,
Horseback Rider

Superpower:

Communicates with
animals

Fear:

Heights

Special Gadget:

Book of Knowledge

Carries:

Book of Knowledge, has
horse named "Spirit"

IMAN

SARA

Sport:

Swimming

Role:

Environmentalist,
Swimmer

Superpower:

Breathes underwater for
a long time

Fear:

Drowning

Special Gadget:

Metal Ball

Carries:

Sunscreen, Water
canteen, Metal Ball

SUPPORTING CHARACTERS

JAFFAR

JASMIN

QUEEN DAYFA

THE JANNAH JEWELS ADVENTURE 9

SYRIA

ARTIFACT 9: WHITE SCARF

"Tie your heart to the Qur'an like a tight knot."
~ Sensei Elle

As salaamu alaikum Dear Readers,

The Jannah Jewels had an awesome adventure in America! They successfully made it out of Mississippi with the 7th and 8th artifacts!

Now, in Book 9, join the Jewels on a brand new mission as they head to beautiful Aleppo, Syria in all its glory and find many great surprises along the way.

They meet the beloved Queen Dayfa Khatun, who demonstrated sincere piety, took great care of her people and was an advocate of learning.

The Jewels discover the value of kindness and develop a deeper love for the Qur'an and each other.

Get ready to find a Surprise in Syria with the Jannah Jewels!

With warmest salaams,
Tayyaba Syed and Umm Nura

Prologue

Long ago, in the ancient Moroccan walled city of Fes, a decision was made. Once the great and peaceful Master Archer had reached old age, he chose an apprentice to take his place and be trusted with the enormous task of protecting the world from the forces of evil. As Master Archer, he carried a deep Secret — one that no one else knew. To keep it hidden, the Secret was written upon a scroll, placed into a box and locked away in a giant Golden Clock. The Master Archer's apprentice had to keep this Golden Clock safe from the hands of evil after him.

He had watched his students of archery very carefully. Two students stood out to him like no other: Layla and Khan. Layla was flawless in her aim and light on her feet, who knew how to focus hard with her vision and heart. She wanted nothing more than to bring peace into the world and use her skills in that way. Khan, on the other hand, was a fierce-fighter with strong hands and swift strategies and worked extra hard to gain his Master's attention. He was an expert archer who learned the art from his older brother Idrees — a highly-trained senior student of the Master's and the one who raised Khan like his own son since they were orphaned as young children.

To everyone's surprise, the old and wise Master Archer chose Layla as his successor, making it the first time in history that a woman was appointed the role. Layla humbly accepted and continued to train relentlessly to prepare for this great task.

"You must carry great humility and selflessness to lead others," the Master Archer told his students. "Only then will you be followed."

Many of the Master's students respected and honored his decision, including Khan. He admired Layla for her nobility and knew she must deserve this honor if the Master had chosen her over him and all the other students. He saw in her qualities he had wanted in a wife and decided to send for her hand in marriage. Layla and her family soon accepted.

After some time, they were blessed with two children: a boy named Jaffar and later a girl named Jasmin. Jaffar was a gentle and curious spirit who loved to practice calligraphy and read as many books as he could. Jasmin was quite the opposite, as she loved to play all kinds of sports, tumble, and practice archery like her mother. The family lived happily together in a villa in the city of Fes and were highly regarded in their community.

Things did not remain peaceful for long, though. After the Master Archer announced his decision, a group of angry and disappointed students banded together and decided to leave the institution. Over time, their anger turned into greed and jealousy. They spread rumors about Khan saying that he only married Layla to gain power and get his hands on the Golden Clock. They devised an evil plan to separate the two great archers and steal the Golden Clock along with its Secret.

One unexpected day, when Khan and his older brother Idrees returned from a business trip to Khan's home, the family was attacked by a group of intruders. They hid in the tall trees surrounding the villa and fired countless arrows wounding Khan. To protect Layla and the Secret of the Golden Clock, Idrees ordered her to escape immediately through a secret passage.

Layla protested and pleaded. She could not imagine leaving her family and home, but Idrees reminded her that as the new Master Archer she had to protect not just her family but the whole world. Being the only one with access to the Secret of the Golden Clock, Layla realized she had to seek safety for the world's sake. Heavy-hearted, she quickly escaped without a trace.

When Khan learned of Layla's disappearance, he blamed Idrees for making her leave. It caused a great rift in their relationship for many years. Khan searched far and wide for his beloved wife but to no avail. With time, he grew angry, bitter and frustrated. He refused to let his children meet their uncle, even though both Jaffar and Jasmin loved Idrees dearly. Despite Khan's resistance, Idrees repeatedly tried to make amends with his little brother as well as stay connected with his niece and nephew, especially since he felt guilty for making them grow up without their mother.

Without Layla's love and tenderness, Jaffar

became serious and distant, while Jasmin turned hard and difficult. The siblings grew apart, developing animosity for each other.

Nothing was ever the same again. Layla's void filled the home with heaviness and disharmony. Where had she gone? Would she ever come back? Will Khan, Idrees, Jaffar and Jasmin ever find peace and happiness again?

1

Awakening

"Peace," Mus'ab greeted Jaffar as he limped into the open courtyard of his house.

"And upon you," replied Jaffar, who sat on a cushioned chair made of bamboo next to a ceramic birdbath.

"My mom sent me to call you for breakfast."

Jaffar looked down at the calligraphy he had scribbled onto a scrap piece of paper. "I'm not really hungry right now," he told Mus'ab softly.

"What? You gotta eat. Mom made your favorite 1,000-hole pancakes, and I just brought home fresh *khobz* from the bakery. Now come."

He grabbed Jaffar's arm to lift him off the chair,

6

but Jaffar kept his weight down.

"I'm serious, Mus'ab," Jaffar said pulling his arm back. "I'm not hungry right now."

Mus'ab took a deep breath. He reluctantly grabbed the closest Ottoman and sat next to Jaffar. "What's up? You obviously don't seem like yourself this morning."

Jaffar kept his gaze down and folded the paper scrap between his fingers. "Nothing," he finally responded.

"Soooo, we can play this game all morning, or you can just tell me what's on your mind. I'm not eating without you."

Jaffar lifted his eyes up slowly. He hesitated before speaking again. "You're not going to understand."

"Try me."

Canaries hovered above the boys' heads pausing every-so-often to drink from the birdbath next to Jaffar. Their constant chirping kept breaking the uncomfortable silence in the air.

"It's been months," Jaffar finally spoke. "I miss my home and my family. I just want things to go back to the way they were!" He tossed the folded paper onto the mosaic tabletop.

Mus'ab picked it up. He slowly opened it and saw the Arabic word '*Abb*' sketched beautifully on the paper.

"I miss my father too," he told Jaffar. "But, unlike yours, mine is gone forever."

Jaffar suddenly sat up taller and leaned in to Mus'ab. "I'm so sorry. I didn't mean to make you feel bad."

"You can't lose hope," said Mus'ab, his curly hair bobbing as he shook his head. "Your father will come out of this, God-willing, and when he does you need to remind him of the beauty of goodness again."

"He became such a different person after Mother left," Jaffar told him. "And then he just became obsessed with defeating the Jannah Jewels. I get so upset just thinking about it." He closed his eyes and rubbed his forehead in frustration.

Mus'ab sat and thought quietly for a few

8

moments. He then stood up and tried to pull Jaffar up by the arm again. "Come on. Let's get some food in you, and then we can head over to the hospital to see your dad. It's been a while since you've gone to see him. You're not going to help him in any way by moping around here hungry and sad."

This time, Jaffar did not resist and willingly joined Mus'ab and his family for breakfast.

*   *   *   *

Jaffar and Mus'ab arrived at Omar Drissi Hospital a few hours after breakfast. They did their usual routine, where Jaffar headed up to see his father while Mus'ab waited in the lobby. As Jaffar stepped out of the elevator, he made a quiet prayer seeking God's help in curing his father back to health and goodness. He could hear his heartbeat drumming against his chest as it was always hard to see his father in such a helpless state. It had been 3 months since his father's concussion had taken over their lives. He took a deep breath as he opened the door and walked into his father's hospital room.

The air was cold and reeked of the familiar

smell of disinfectants. Jaffar's eyes went straight to the bed. It was empty. His heart began to beat even faster as he looked around the small room in a panic.

Where could he have gone? worried Jaffar. He rushed out of the room straight to the nurses' desk.

"Excuse me! I'm looking for my father in room 431! His name is Khan! He was in here for a concussion and was kept sedated due to his amnesia outbursts, but now he's not in his room!" Jaffar panted through his words as he spoke to the staff.

A head nurse wearing *hijab* stared at Jaffar sympathetically. "We've been wondering when you'd come back to see your father. You'll be happy to know that he's doing much better, and we took him off the heavy medications. Your sister was wheeling him around to give him a change of scenery. They should be back soon. I told her to have him back here in time for his lunch."

A sudden feeling of relief and joy came over Jaffar. He could not believe what the nurse just told him. He decided to go look for them.

"Do you have any idea where I could find them?"

he questioned the nurse.

"She may have taken him to the hospital gardens. Just look for the signs," she pointed behind him.

Jaffar rushed down the stairs without a second thought. He followed the signs leading him to the courtyard of the hospital. As he approached the glass doors that opened to the gardens, he saw his sister's gray *hijab* flowing in the wind behind her. She stood behind a wheelchair, and there, Jaffar saw Khan's head from the back. They were stationed next to a white, porcelain fountain.

"Father!" Jaffar shouted as he ran through the automatic doors. He felt like a little kid again who used to run into his father's arms after he returned from a business trip. Jaffar wanted to leap into Khan's lap and just tell him how much he loved him and missed him, but then something came over him. He realized he was older now, and they were different people.

"Jaffar? Is that you?" a frail Khan looked up at his son for the first time in months.

Jaffar fell to the ground, threw his head into his

11

father's lap and cried. "You're okay! You're okay, Father," he wept. "And you know who I am! You know who I am!"

Khan laid a cold hand on Jaffar's head. "How can I forget?"

"I just want things to go back to the way they were. I know you changed after Mother left. I will do whatever it takes to find her and bring her back to us," Jaffar shook as he spoke through his tears, his head still in his father's lap.

He then felt another hand on him, this time on his shoulder and warmer. He looked up and saw Jasmin smiling down at him.

"Let's find her…together."

2

New Mission

Iman's eyes looked as if they would pop out of her head while she flipped through the large, colorful pages of *The Great Book of Animals*, her recent gift from Master Rider. There was so much information to be absorbed. However, she kept her main focus on how to communicate with horses, since she wanted to develop a stronger relationship with her horse Spirit.

"Can you get your nose out of that book already and watch me do my Ollie?" Jaide whined as she clumsily practiced the trick on her electric skateboard.

Iman peeked over the top of her book not looking very amused. "I've seen you do it a hundred times.

What's the big deal?"

"It's not as easy on this electric board," answered Jaide. "Did you happen to see how many times I fell? It's like starting all over again." With frustration, Jaide popped the board with one foot to lift it up and then wiped the sweat off her forehead. She then walked over to where Iman was sitting on a nearby bench.

Iman closed her book and stood up. "I'm not trying to ignore you, you know? Becoming a better horseback rider is just as important to me as improving your skateboarding skills is to you," Iman clarified.

"I just need you to tell me what I'm doing wrong," said Jaide. "Hidayah told me that she senses our next mission is approaching soon, and I want to be super ready."

It had been two months since the Jannah Jewels had been back in Vancouver from their last mission in America. No one knew for sure when Sensei Elle would send them off on their next mission.

Iman could see a look of desperation in Jaide's small brown eyes. She tilted her head lazily to one side and crossed her arms over her chest. "Okay. Let's see it."

Jaide took a deep breath and walked a few feet back. She adjusted her helmet, which was slightly crooked on top of the *hijab* on her head. She positioned herself carefully on her board, keeping her weight even in the middle. As the board picked up speed, Jaide bent her knees forward and kept her focus on the upcoming hump in the skate park where she was aiming to do her Ollie. The four fast-spinning wheels scraped against the concrete getting louder and louder as she neared Iman.

As soon as Jaide approached the hump, she lifted her arms in the air behind her, squatted down and pressing her left foot into the tail of the skateboard tilting it upwards, and jumped full force with the board into the air as if it was glued to her sneakers.

Iman watched as Jaide soared high up over the hump free as a bird. She smiled with anticipation thinking Jaide would have a smooth landing, but to her surprise, Jaide pounded onto the ground hard, tripped over her board and rolled continuously on the pavement while the electric skateboard zoomed towards Iman.

"Oh no!" screamed Iman. As the board charged towards her, she reacted quickly by stepping onto it with force and brought it to a halt. Then with the board in her arms, she ran towards Jaide who was planted face down on the ground. "Jaide, are you okay?"

Jaide slowly looked up. She could only make out Iman's towering silhouette with the afternoon sun blazing above her.

"I'm alive," she moaned with pain.

Iman bent down to help lift up her friend. Jaide weakly stood up looking deflated.

"Man, I'm just getting worse with each try. Practice meets pavement," she whimpered.

"I saw what you did wrong. It's basic physics."

"Oh, God. Please don't tell me this is going to be a science lesson," said Jaide rolling her eyes.

"You want my help or not?" Iman asked sternly.

"Fine."

Holding the board flat in front of her face, Iman pointed to its tail. "So, your launch was perfect, but your landing was all off."

"The scrapes on my knees can tell you that."

"Just listen. Will ya?" said Iman impatiently. "While in the air, you're forgetting to slide your front foot forward to level your board out. That's why when you land, you end up putting all your weight on the tail of your board which sends you flying off it."

Jaide let out a heavy sigh and dropped her head. "Whatever. I give up."

Iman gave her a hard stare. "What? No way! Do you remember how you led us with your board in Constantinople? Get yourself back in that mindset. You can do anything you put your mind to," said Iman.

"Nah. I'm in too much pain. Part of me just wants to go back to my old manual skateboard." She glanced over to her bag off to the side with the edge of her old red skateboard sticking out of it.

18

"You can't! That's Mus'ab's now! You promised to bring it back to him."

This was not like Jaide at all.

"What's wrong with you? You can do this! Now go!" Iman shoved the electric board into Jaide's limp arms and pushed her back to the starting point.

Sluggishly, Jaide dragged her feet back to the opposite end of the park. She mustered up whatever energy she had left and climbed back onto her board. "I can do this," she whispered to herself. Then with a loud "*Bismillah!*" she took off again towards the hump.

"Go, Jaide, go!" Iman cheered.

Just as Jaide was about to reach the hump, she saw Hidayah and Sara riding frantically atop Spirit out of the tall trees towards her and Iman. She then quickly maneuvered around the hump instead of doing the Ollie, yanked her bag off the ground and pulled Iman onto the board with her.

"Ahh! What are you doing? Where are we going?" Iman clumsily positioned herself, grabbing hold of Jaide's shoulder with one hand and gripping her animal book with the other. After being disoriented for a minute, Iman caught sight of Hidayah and Sara on horseback.

"Jaide! Iman!" Hidayah called out. "We've been looking all over for you guys!"

The four Jannah Jewels gathered together next to a patch of tall grass as they tried to catch their breaths.

"Is everything okay?" Iman asked with worry looking up at Hidayah and Sara.

"Sensei summoned us to the dojo right away," answered Sara. Her cheeks were moist and flushed with color.

"Oh no! You think it's time for the next mission?" questioned Jaide. "I am so not ready. It's like I forgot how to skateboard."

Hidayah gave Jaide a puzzled look. "You forgot how to ride your skateboard? I just saw what you did back there with your board, bag and Iman. It looks like you still got it to me."

Sara nodded in agreement. "Yes, you're fine.

Now let's go."

"But…" Jaide tried to tell them about her Ollie.

"You'll be fine, Jaide," Iman softly encouraged from behind. "We have Allah to help us always. Just put your trust back in Him.

Jaide kept her gaze forward and stayed quiet.

Hidayah nudged Spirit with her legs and pulled the right rein to steer him back. The four Jewels raced through the woodlands as the sun's rays seeped through the canopy of the tall trees. They then headed up a nearby hill to their Sensei's dojo.

As they came to a stop, Sara disbanded Spirit first. Right away, she heard a faint sound coming from within the dojo.

"Shhh," she quickly quieted the others as they set foot on the grassy floor. "Do you guys hear that?"

All of their ears stood up to listen.
"When I was far away,
and Qur'an seemed to me a foreign book.
I knew I was astray,
but didn't even want to take a look.

I forced myself one day,
to test the things they say,
and ever since that day,
I am addicted to Qur'an."

"Is that Sensei singing?" Jaide asked with wonderment.

The Jewels' eyes lit up.

"Yes!" realized Hidayah. "She sounds so beautiful. Listen."

"When I'm feeling sore
and darkness heavily weighs upon my heart.
When I can take no more,
I feel depleted and worn and need a new start.
I quickly wash and race to some quiet place.
I seek a special peace one only finds in the Qur'an.
Page after page,
line after line,
each day I find new wonders in Qur'an.
Page after page,

*line after line, *

each day I find my life enlightened by Qur'an."

"That song…," Sara's voice trailed off. "It's so touching," she whispered with tears sparkling in her eyes.

"Yeah it is," agreed Iman.

"*Achoo!*" Jaide sneezed loudly. "*Alhamdullilah!*"

"Jaide! Could you be any louder?" Iman asked startled.

Sensei's singing had suddenly stopped.

"Sor-ry! It must be all this pollen flying around," Jaide attempted to explain her outburst.

"*As salaamu alaikum*," Sensei Elle greeted as she met the Jewels outside. She looked radiant in her red robe and *hijab* as the sun shined on her face.

"*Walaikum as salaam*," they all replied.

"I'm glad all of you made it. The time has come for your next mission," she told them calmly.

Sara's heart was still feeling the effect of Sensei's song. "Sensei?" she suddenly spoke up. "May I ask you something?"

Sensei nodded.

"That song that you were singing...where is it from?"

Sensei gave her a warm smile. "It's from where you are headed next."

"And where's that, Sensei?" Hidayah jumped on the opportunity to find out.

"Syria," Sensei answered with contentment.

A feeling of calmness came over Sara. "My father was raised there," she told everyone. "He always talks about how beautiful it was and how it was such an amazing part of his life."

"As it was mine," said Sensei. "And now each of you will get to experience its beauty and richness, God-willing."

Hidayah liked the idea of knowing a piece of Sensei's past. She felt as if it deepened their connection. She then took a moment to look at each of her best friends. She realized it had been a long time since she saw a sense of peace on their faces before heading out to a new mission.

Sensei pulled out two small paperback books from inside the bell sleeve of her robe. She handed one to Hidayah and one to Sara.

"These will help you on your mission along with all your other tools," she told the girls, who flipped through the books inquisitively.

"What are they?" questioned Iman.

"They're songbooks," answered Sara confidently.

"Yes," affirmed Sensei. "Use them like maps."

"Maps?" Jaide asked with confusion.

"You will understand with time. Remember to also rely on the *Qur'an* for guidance as it will bring you relief and peace when you need it most. The best way to do that is to tie your heart to the *Qur'an* like a tight knot. Now go. You must get on your way at once," she instructed.

A look of sudden concern came over Hidayah. "Wait. You're not going to walk us down to the time-traveling maple tree?"

Sensei stood quietly for a moment. "You'll find

me eventually," she then informed them.

The Jannah Jewels were each puzzled by Sensei's words and glared at each other with bunched eyebrows.

"Can you tell us what artifact we are looking for, Sensei?" asked Sara.

"You need to find the flags of faith that can be fastened together."

Jaide scratched her head. "Does Syria have more than one national flag?"

"May God cover each of you with goodness. Peace be with you all," and with those words, Sensei gracefully walked back into the dojo.

"Sensei!" Jaide called out in desperation. "Can you please elaborate on that some more?" but Sensei was gone. Jaide grunted hard. "Why can't we for once just leave for a mission with all the information in hand?" she complained.

Iman gave her a hard stare. "Are you okay? Did you skip lunch or something?"

As Jaide opened her mouth to answer, Sara

quickly chimed in.

"Umm…how hard can it be to find some flags?" she sounded very optimistic. "Plus, what fun would it be if we knew exactly what to do?"

"Don't forget that I have my ancient map," reassured Hidayah. "We'll look at it once we get to our destination. For now, we need to get to the maple tree right away."

Each of the Jewels gathered her belongings and prepared to head back down the grassy hill.

"I'm going to bring my horse this time," Iman walked up to Spirit and carefully lifted herself onto his saddle.

"Sara, you ride with Iman. Jaide, I'll ride with you. Let's go!" ordered Hidayah.

The other Jewels did as Hidayah said without uttering another word. As they rode down the hill, blades of green grass flattened underneath them. The ride to the maple tree felt heavy to Hidayah.

Oh God, you are closer to us than our jugular vein. Please keep our hearts focused on You, and our bond close for Your Sake, she quietly prayed.

Jaide slowed her board down as they neared their favorite maple tree. The Jannah Jewels played together here for years before they learned of its hidden secret. They loved any opportunity to come back to it.

"Everyone ready?" Hidayah asked as she stood at the back of Jaide's board. She turned and looked up at Iman and Sara atop Spirit.

"Yes," they all hummed.

"Okay. On three. One...two..."

Suddenly, Jaide felt the urge to sneeze again. She let out a loud 'achoo!' causing her to press against the tree trunk to stay balanced on her board. Before she knew it, the trunk opened launching Hidayah and her down a long, dark tunnel.

"*Bismillaaaaaaaaah!*" screamed Hidayah.

Iman and Sara watched as their two friends disappeared into the trunk of the tree.

"Oh no! They left without us!" Iman panicked.

"Hurry! We all need to leave at the same time!"

Sara nudged Iman from the back.

"Okay. Okay. Stay calm, and let's quickly say the *Bismillah* together. Iman took a deep breath. "Close your eyes. Ready?"

"Yes!"

Then in unison, Iman and Sara recited, "*Bismillah hir Rahman nir Raheem.*"

3

Separation

"Where are we?" asked Jaide as she rubbed her head from the hard fall.

Hidayah opened her eyes to a star-lit dome. It was nighttime. She slowly lifted herself to a sitting position.

"Are you okay?" she asked Jaide.

"Yes, *Alhamdullilah*."

"What happened?" wondered Hidayah.

Jaide inched herself closer. "I don't know. One second you were doing the countdown. The next second, I sneezed and wound us here under this almond tree."

Suddenly, Hidayah remembered them falling down the maple tree trunk. "Wait. Where are Iman and Sara?!" She painfully crawled around the rocky pavement in search of them.

"No! Could it be?" Jaide asked in realization.

"What?!" Hidayah questioned her.

"Did we leave —without them?!"

*   *   *   *

Iman felt like she was back in Fes, Morocco, when the Jannah Jewels had been split up. However, this time, she did not know anyone in this new place nor where to even begin looking for Jaide and Hidayah. How will they be able to find them without any way to contact them?

Spirit's hooves clamored against the unpaved road leaving a trail of dust behind them as Iman and Sara searched the open land. Sara shielded her eyes from the bright morning sun looking right, left and back for Hidayah and Jaide.

"Where could they have gone?" she shouted to Iman as Spirit galloped into the unknown.

"I don't know!" Iman yelled back. "I don't see them anywhere!"

"I think we should turn around and go back to the almond tree orchard," Sara advised.

Iman yanked Spirit's reins hard. He gradually reduced his speed eventually coming to a full stop.

"Do you see that?" asked Iman.

Sara looked in the direction Iman was staring. Through the haze of the desert heat, Sara could make out hills and homes with a giant castle-looking structure atop a central hill surrounded by a massive brick wall. The city was glowing white.

"It's like the city came out of nowhere," Sara uttered with wonderment.

Iman lifted her glasses off her nose and squinted her eyes. "It's not a mirage, is it?"

"No, I see it too. You think they are there?" asked Sara.

"Where else could they be? We just rode through barren land and found nothing."

Sara took a deep breath. "How long do you think

it will take us to get there?"

"My guess is that it's a 15-minute ride if Spirit can gallop all the way there." Iman rubbed the side of Spirit's neck. She could feel his pulse racing through his hide. "He's going to need some water and food, though, to gain some more energy."

Sara carefully dismounted the horse and removed the canteen from her waist belt. She flipped open its lid and slowly poured water into Spirit's mouth. He released hot, wet air through his giant nostrils sprinkling drops onto her. She laughed with delight.

"Thanks. I needed to cool down anyway," Sara spoke to Spirit. She then removed an apple from her cross-body pouch. "We need you to stay strong for us, Spirit. God-willing, we'll get through this." She stroked his mane as he crunched the fruit loudly between his massive teeth.

"How are you so calm right now?"

Sara lifted her head up to meet Iman's eyes, but they were hidden behind her sun-tinted glasses.

"We're in Syria," Sara smiled faintly. "My heart

feels at ease here."

"But we're separated from Hidayah and Jaide. Hidayah always leads us and is the one with the ancient map and compass, while Jaide's time-travelling watch helps us get home in time," Iman breathed heavy as she wiped her forehead with the back of her hand.

"We haven't always relied on those tools, Iman," Sara reminded her. "Remember back in Constantinople, we had none of those." As she fastened her canteen back onto her waist belt, she noticed the songbook from Sensei. It was nicely rolled and inserted into one of her belt straps. "Hey, and we have the songbook!"

Iman bent down to read over Sara's shoulder as she sifted through its pages. Her eyes fell upon a song called "Evanescence."

Sara read the verses outloud,
"For every start, there is an end.
In every road, there comes a bend.
And parting steals your dearest friend."

She paused here. "That's us!"

"Keep reading," Iman instructed her.

"Oh, when will my hurt ever mend?
For every 'open,' there comes a 'closed.'
And every bud will wilt a rose.
And raging storms, they say come after pause.
Most nice things don't last.
The state you're in now's becoming part of the past.
Nothing is constant.
Nothing remains.
Heed the only One you need."

Iman placed her hand on Sara's shoulder. "God is always with us," she realized. "That's how we get through our missions."

Sara climbed back onto Spirit's back. "*Bismillah.* Let's go then."

Iman took a deep breath and then said a silent prayer. *Oh Allah, let this city be full of blessings for us and make it easy for us to find help along the way as You are always with us.*

With a slight tap of her heel, Iman nudged Spirit to lurch forward. He quickly picked up speed and thundered towards the ancient white city. Sara held on tight to Iman, keeping her face shielded behind Iman's back from the clouds of dust accumulating around them. Nothing seemed to bother Sara now. She was in Syria. She was home.

4

Truth

Uncle Idrees' house had been a home for Jasmin these last few months. He had been there for her before and after her surgery for her broken arm. As she and Jaffar walked through the narrow Moroccan streets, she wondered how her uncle would react seeing the two of them together again.

"I don't understand why he didn't tell me that Father had recovered," Jaffar interrupted her thought as they stepped on the stoned doorstep.

"I thought he would have told you right away," she replied as she scratched an annoying itch under her heavy arm cast. "He knew about your whereabouts. I didn't."

Jaffar glanced at the neon cast covering her left arm. "How long do you have to wear that?"

"Another month." Jasmin rolled her eyes. "I can't wait to get it off. I miss archery so much."

"Jazz," Jaffar's voice was low. "I'm sorry – about everything."

She looked at him sincerely. "I already forgave you right before I went into surgery. I forgave everyone. Even…Mother…and even…the Jannah Jewels. I can't describe to you how scary it was for me to have no one with me before the surgery except for Uncle Idrees. I made so many prayers before they put me to sleep. I'm tired of all the fighting. I just want things to go back to the way they were. I want Mother back. I want Father to be healthy and happy again. I just want us to be a family again, God-willing."

There was a lump in Jaffar's throat. He remained quiet and nodded in agreement.

Jasmin knocked on the large wooden door and waited to see who would answer. The two siblings heard the locks unfasten from behind the door. Uncle

39

Idrees suddenly appeared in front of them. His eyes grew big with surprise.

"Jaffar! Jasmin! You're here...together?!" He grabbed his niece and nephew into a strong bear hug. "All Praise is for Allah! Not a day goes by that I don't pray for you two!" He rested his head between their shoulders. Jaffar and Jasmin could feel his tears seep through their garments. They turned their heads towards each other and smiled.

"Yes, we're here together, Uncle," Jaffar spoke up. "We needed to see you."

Their uncle slowly pulled himself back from them and wiped the wetness from his eyes. "Come in. Come in. This is a moment to celebrate!" Uncle Idrees took hold of their hands and walked them into the courtyard of his house. He led them to a corner with lawn sofas and chairs full of colorful cushions. "Have a seat. Let me get your Aunt Nur. She'll be thrilled to see you both together again."

"We'd like to just talk to you alone first, Uncle," Jaffar intercepted. Jasmin noticed his eyes wander around the shaded courtyard with nostalgia. It had been years since Jaffar had set foot in his uncle's home. Ever since his mother had disappeared, Khan refused to let him and Jasmin come visit Uncle Idrees.

Uncle Idrees adjusted the small rimless cap on his bald head. His expression grew concerned. "Is everything okay? How's Khan?" He positioned his stout body onto one of the cushioned lawn chairs. Jaffar and Jasmin then sat down.

"Yes, he's fine. *Alhamdullilah*," Jaffar softly answered back. "Uncle? Why didn't you inform me of his recovery?" he suddenly questioned him.

His uncle quickly lowered his gaze and hesitated to reply as if searching for words. "I wanted you to come see for yourself," stuttered Uncle Idrees.

Jaffar bunched his eyebrows together. "And what if I didn't go by the hospital for days or weeks?"

"But you did go," Uncle Idrees smirked.

A long exhale escaped Jasmin. "Uncle Idrees, there's something you're not telling us, and we're here to find out. Were you trying to keep Jaffar away from Father?" Her face was flushed and serious.

41

Beads of sweat gathered over Uncle Idrees' forehead, some dripping down his sideburns. He pulled out a handkerchief from his robe's pocket and wiped his face profusely. "Why would you two think such a thing?"

"Because that's what it seems like you did!" Jaffar's voice grew loud, and his cheeks turned red.

Uncle Idrees glanced between their faces. "Your father doesn't know that you've been helping the Jannah Jewels, Jaffar," he finally spoke up. "I was afraid it may upset his recovery."

Jaffar sat puzzled, as his eyebrows furrowed as they always did when he was confused or in deep thought.

"You probably don't remember, but years ago, your parents were attacked by some intruders."

Jasmin's face immediately turned pale. "Yes. I remember," she painfully recalled hiding in a crawlspace to protect her and Jaffar per Uncle Idrees' order when they were little. When he finally came to retrieve them, everything had changed. Their father had been rushed to the hospital and was never the same after that, while their mother had left them unexpectedly. It's a memory that haunts Jasmin to this day. Her gray eyes sparkled with tears.

Uncle Idrees placed his hand gently on her head. "I'm sorry."

She looked at him puzzled. "What are you sorry for?" Jasmin questioned.

The lawn chair creaked against the tiled-floor as Uncle Idrees stood up. He paced around them for some time.

"I am the one that made your mother escape the attackers," his voice was low and shaky. "Layla was appointed as the new Master Archer. She had a great responsibility to protect the Golden Clock and its Secret from evil hands. It was the only choice." Uncle Idrees avoided eye contact with Jasmin and Jaffar. "Your father was devastated and made it his mission to find her, but he never could."

The two siblings listened attentively, their faces solemn and meek.

"But that still doesn't explain his greed for the Golden Clock's Secret or going after the Jannah

Jewels," Jaffar wondered.

Uncle Idrees met Jaffar's eyes. "When he wasn't able to find her, he decided he would send you two on missions searching for the ancient artifacts. He figured if he finds the Clock, he'll find her," he told them as he stroked his small, white beard. He then continued, "When the Jannah Jewels started showing up on the same missions, he assumed they must be working for the intruders. Khan wanted to stop them at all cost, even though I advised him to leave them alone. He had lost all trust in me, though, since your mother left."

Jasmin shot up out of her chair abruptly. "The Jannah Jewels are working for Mother, aren't they?"

Jaffar glared hard at his uncle. "Are they?" he spoke stunned.

"Your mother must remain safe and unharmed," Uncle Idrees said firmly. "No one must find her – not even the two of you."

"You didn't answer my question! Are the Jannah Jewels working for Mother?" Jaffar pried. "You know where she is! You need to tell us! Please!" He was

44

standing now and panting as he pleaded.

Uncle Idrees turned his back towards them. "You need to leave now."

"You've known the truth all this time," Jaffar uttered with disappointment. "How could you do this to us? How could you keep us apart from our mother and see your own brother suffer for the last 5 years?" Jaffar's heart ached as he held back his tears. "You're not who I thought you were at all!"

The air was silent. Uncle Idrees kept his back towards them.

"So that's it? You're not going to tell us where to find her?" Jasmin's blood was now racing through her veins. "You only took care of me at the hospital out of guilt!" Jasmin's words came out like spit. "Let's go, Jaffar. We'll find Mother on our own," Jasmin grabbed him by the hand leading him out of the courtyard.

"Children, you musn't!" Uncle Idrees suddenly turned and ran after them.

Jaffar turned back, his eyes red with fury. "You've kept her away from us long enough!" he cried. "Don't try to stop us now!"

And with that, Jasmin yanked her brother forward and out of their uncle's house – neither of them wanted to ever set foot in that house again.

5

Lost and Found

The old houses made of stucco and bricks were narrow and tall lined up right next to each other. Hidayah and Jaide aimlessly walked through the dimly-lit neighborhood streets not knowing where to go. The cool air was calm around them. They walked past street carts that were covered with thick cloths to protect goods for the night and saw many stray cats looking for scraps.

"I wish we had Sara's metal ball," said Jaide. "We could really use that flashlight."

Hidayah looked up at the moonlit sky. The moon was aglow and looked as familiar as always. It gave her a sense of peace. She wondered if Sara and

Iman were looking at the same moon as her.

"We should find a place to rest for the night," she suggested to Jaide. "There's no use wandering in the dark."

Jaide let out a deep sigh. "This is all my fault. If I hadn't had my untimely sneeze, we wouldn't have been in this whole mess."

Hidayah stepped closer to Jaide. "The sneeze was out of your control. I'm sure this all happened for a reason. We're meant to be here." She carefully examined the houses along the pebbled road, some with canopied shops on the ground floor. She then noticed one particular house that was slightly bigger than the others. It had a fairly large doorstep with potted plants in front of it. "Let's just lay right there." She pointed out the step to Jaide.

"What if the owner gets upset at us?" worried Jaide.

"We'll just rest here until daybreak," Hidayah reassured her. "As soon as there is some sunlight, we can start searching for Sara and Iman again."

The two friends situated themselves on the

doorstep and leaned their backs against the front door. They raised their legs up close to their chests using their knees as pillows. Despite the uncomfortable surface, Hidayah and Jaide said their nightly supplications and fell fast asleep.

*   *   *   *

Hidayah felt as if she had slept for hours, but it was still dark out. A familiar voice had stirred her awake. She slowly lifted her head up to listen. Her body ached and was stiff from sleeping upright, so she carefully stood up. The windows of the house were open, and Hidayah could hear the *Qur'an* being recited.

What time is it? Hidayah wondered. The streets were still empty and quiet, and the sky leaked a thin thread of white. *Dawn must be near*, she realized.

She looked down at Jaide, who was still sound asleep. Hidayah gently shook her awake.

"Jaide. Jaide," she whispered. "Wake up. Let's go. I hear someone inside." Jaide was in a deep sleep and not responding. Hidayah shook her harder. "Jaide! Wake up!" This time, her whisper was more like a soft yell.

"What? Where are we?" A startled Jaide abruptly sprouted up. She immediately lost her balance, knocking over one of the potted plants.

"Shh! You're going to wake up the neighborhood!"

"Aww, man. I'm covered in dirt."

"How did you fall?"

"My foot fell asleep," explained Jaide, who was now more awake than ever. "It's still tingling with numbness."

Hidayah noticed right away that the voice had stopped reciting *Qur'an*. Then both girls noticed a light turn on from within the house.

"Uh oh! Let's get out of here!" Jaide said trying to lift herself back up but not fast enough with her sleeping foot. "Ow! Ow! Ow!" She hopped on one foot to avoid falling again.

"We can't leave now! You broke their pot!" Hidayah reminded her.

"What if it's a big, angry uncle that lives here? Wake up, foot! Wake UP!" She lifted her sneaker and shook her foot.

Suddenly, the locks on the other side of the door unfastened, and the door swung open. A young teenage girl stood in front of Hidayah and Jaide. She wore a long white pull-over *hijab* over a white prayer skirt. Her face was hard to see in the darkness.

No one spoke a word. The girls stood frozen.

"Peace be upon you both."

Hidayah and Jaide exchanged a quick glance at one another.

"Peace be upon you too," Hidayah finally spoke up. "We apologize for knocking over your plant here."

The girl looked down at the splattered dirt and broken dried clay.

"Oh. That's what that noise was. Are you okay?"

"Yes," replied Jaide. "I'm so sorry. I was really sleepy."

"Well, you must be after such a long journey. Please come in. We weren't expecting you so early this morning."

Before the girls could clarify, she had already

turned and walked back into the house.

"What do we do?" whispered Jaide.

Hidayah shrugged her shoulders. "Let's at least tell her we aren't who she thinks we are."

They slowly entered the house and removed their shoes in the corridor. Hidayah noticed a peacefulness immediately surround her. She and Jaide followed the girl into a large open room with a high-ceiling, plush carpets, tall roped curtains and foam cushions lined along the walls and floor. Lamps and lanterns were dimly lit around the space, and beautiful chandeliers hung above them.

Then it dawned on Hidayah. *Electricity*. Did we arrive in the present again? she thought to herself.

She leaned in close to Jaide's ear and whispered her realization. Jaide's mouth flew open. She nodded slowly in agreement to Hidayah.

"What are your names?" the girl asked as she brought a tray with small glasses of mint tea on it. The visor of her *hijab* created a shadow over her face.

"I'm Hidayah, and this is Jaide." The two of them sat and drank the tea contently. It reminded Hidayah so much of the mint tea Sensei Elle had taught her to make.

"You must really like archery," the girl said to Hidayah, noticing the bow hung over her back.

"Yes, it's my favorite sport."

"Mine too," the girl told them smiling big. "Next summer my teachers are sending me to an archery academy in Morocco, God-willing. They say it's been around for centuries and only the most gifted students graduate from the program."

"That sounds amazing," said Jaide with astonishment.

The girl placed herself on the carpet near them and adjusted her *hijab* back. A lamp's light glowed against her skin, making her gray eyes shine bright.

Hidayah and Jaide almost dropped their tea glasses out of their hands.

"Sensei?" Hidayah asked in shock.

The girl suddenly chuckled. "Sensei? Are you

kidding? I'm too young to be a sensei. You can call me 'Elle' – that's what my friends call me."

6

Help Along the Way

The ride to the white city was shorter than what Iman had predicted. As they drew closer, they found an area that looked like a rest stop.

"Let's stop here?" asked Iman. She led Spirit to the right off the main road. Many travelers were moving in and out of the open courtyard. There were horsemen and camel-riders scattered about eating, drinking and socializing, while their mounts drank from watering holes and grazed on hay and grass. A few feet away, Iman saw a ranch-style building with many doors and windows.

Spirit started grazing right away. The girls dismounted the tired horse and tethered him on a pole.

Sara stretched her limbs as she inhaled deeply. "It's so peaceful here," she noted.

"I don't think Hidayah and Jaide are here," guessed Iman. "This looks like an inn or something for travelers."

"It would be a long trek for them to cover on Jaide's electric skateboard. What if they arrived at a different tree than us? Or what if they landed somewhere else in the city since they left slightly before us?" Sara's mind was racing with possibilities.

Iman's face was deep in thought. "Let's ask someone where we are and if they saw two other girls our age come through here," she then suggested. "Once we have some information, I can do some research with my *Book of Knowledge* and get some direction.

The ground began to shake as a large caravan entered the rest stop with numerous camels carrying goods of all kinds.

"Wow, look at that caravan! Where do you think it's from?" Sara wondered.

"I don't know. Let's go find out."

The girls ran to meet the head of the caravan. He was an elderly man with sun-dried skin behind a white beard, who was tying his camel and directing his men where to let the other camels rest.

"Don't leave your camel's side!" he shouted at the other riders. One-by-one, each camel kneeled and then sat and grazed while its rider dismounted. No one seemed to really notice Iman and Sara as they walked past them.

"Greetings of Peace, Sir," Iman greeted the old man. "We were wondering if you could tell us where we are exactly right now."

The man looked down at the girls as he cleared his throat.

"How did you end up here in the first place?" The wrinkles on his face stretched as he talked.

"We got separated from our travel companions," Sara quickly answered. "We were hoping to find them here, but we didn't. We think they may have entered that big city up ahead with the big castle on the hill."

With the tail end of his turban, the man wiped his sweaty face. He then used it like a fan to cool off his skin.

"That's actually a citadel. The castle is a just a section of it," he corrected.

Iman itched to grab her *Book of Knowledge* to learn more about what a citadel is but knew she'd have to wait. Instead, she just nodded as if she understood what he was saying.

"And this is a caravansary for travelers."

"It's quite busy," Sara stated.

"Yes, and our caravan just made it busier," the man laughed.

"Where are you headed?" questioned Sara.

He examined their faces for a few moments before responding. "This is our final stop on the Silk Road."

Both girls were taken aback. "The Silk Road?!" they asked simultaneously.

The old man stroked the mustache of his beard and stared at the girls. "Yes, why are you so surprised?"

Sara nudged Iman slightly. "Oh! Because we thought we had completely gone the wrong way. Thank Allah, we didn't." She released an uncomfortable smile as she squinted from the sun's brightness.

He glared at them suspiciously. "How do you two plan on entering the city of Halab anyway?"

"We don't know. Could you help us?" Iman asked sincerely.

"It will cost you."

They were not expecting the man to charge them. Iman grew worried as they had no money on them. "How much?" she questioned.

His big, black eyes landed on Sara's canteen. "I want that water vessel. On all my travel, I have never seen one like this before. It will be quite useful on my long journeys."

"Please take it," Sara offered without hesitation. She went to unsnap it off her waist belt.

"I will…after I have safely gotten you to your

destination." He gave the girls a subtle grin. "Once my men and their mounts gain back some energy, we'll be on our way. You may ride alongside the front of the caravan with me."

"May God reward you," thanked Sara. "Could you tell us your name?"

"Abu Yahya."

"Thank you, Abu Yahya," said Iman.

The girls walked back to check on Spirit. As they neared him, Iman pulled out her *Book of Knowledge* from her satchel.

"Okay, so he gave us some big clues as to where and when we have arrived. Now let's do some research before we head out." Iman and Sara sat on the edge of a short, broken brick wall near Spirit.

"The first clue was 'citadel,'" Sara remembered. I like the sound of that word: 'ci-ta-del,' 'ci-ta-del,' ci-ta-del.'"

Iman gave her a hard stare. "Can we focus please?"

Sara giggled. "Ci-ta-del."

"Stop it!"

"Sorry. What does it mean?"

After running through a few spellings through her head, Iman finally found the word in the index.

"A citadel is the defensive core of a town or city. It may consist of a fortress, castle, or a fortified center. It means 'little city,' because it is a smaller part of the bigger city it protects," Iman read.

"There's nothing funny about that," Sara realized.

"No kidding."

"What do you think this city needs to be protected from?"

Iman adjusted her glasses higher up onto the bridge of her nose. "What did Abu Yahya say the name of the city was?"

"Wasn't it Halab or something?"

There were a bunch of different cities pictured under the word 'citadel.' Iman slid her finger down the list of names in search of one named 'Halab.'

"That's odd. The one that matches this location is not named Halab," she pointed out to Sara.

"Aleppo?" Sara read out loud. She looked up towards the city to double check. "Could that really be Aleppo? Oh mi gosh! That does look like the picture in your book. Maybe Halab is another name for it. Go on. Check the next clue then. He said we are in a caravansary."

Iman then flipped through the pages to find out more about that.

"A caravansary is an inn with a central courtyard for travelers in the desert regions of Asia or North Africa."

"Look!" Sara spotted a footnote at the bottom of the page. "Caravansaries were highly used on the ancient Silk Road, which was a network of trade routes through regions of the Asian continent connecting the West and East from China to the Mediterranean Sea, ending at the city of Aleppo (Halab in Arabic)." She placed both her hands on Iman's shoulders and shook her. "We are totally in the right place! Do you realize where we are? We are about to enter the ancient city of Aleppo! I can barely breathe. This is so exciting!"

Iman laughed seeing Sara giddy as can be.

"This is the city my father grew up in and has told me about all his life. We get to see it. We actually get to see it for ourselves…in all its glory. Can you believe it?"

"I wonder what year it is," Iman said nervously all of a sudden as she read more information about Aleppo's history. "It says in 1138, the city was ravaged by one of the deadliest earthquakes in recorded history, and in 1260, it was taken over by the Mongols."

"The Mongols?!" Sara freaked. "The same people who destroyed the House of Wisdom and took over Baghdad?"

"Yup. That was in 1258."

"Oh man. Let's go ask Abu Yahya. If an earthquake or the Mongols are coming, then I change my mind. We need to get out of here A.S.A.P.!" Sara got up and untied Spirit.

She and Iman then quickly walked back to Abu Yahya pulling Spirit behind them. Abu Yahya and his men were gearing up.

"That's a beautiful horse," he said looking up at Spirit.

"Thank you. He was a gift from my father," Iman told him.

"Your father knows a good Arabian horse then." He handed each of the girls a knotted handkerchief in the shape of a small sack. "Here. Have some dates. They will help restore your energy."

Iman and Sara graciously accepted and ate the soft, ripe fruits to their hearts' content. While enjoying the sweet dates, they forgot to ask what year it was. They set out with the caravan reciting quiet supplications along the way for protection and ease. It was the first time they had joined a caravan on their missions. The swaying of the camels seemed rhythmic to the Jewels.

The Mediterranean sun rose to its zenith point as they entered the grand white city, encircled by numerous hills and full of glowing domes and towering minarets. The caravan approached a giant, covered souk with many vendors and shoppers hustling and bustling within it.

"Are you trading goods here?" Iman turned and asked Abu Yahya.

"No, this caravan is not selling any goods," he replied. He then signaled his men to start unloading the camels.

The girls were surprised to see the men then take different items like fabrics, nuts, and pottery and distribute them to various stone homes surrounding the marketplace.

"Who are they giving these to?" asked Sara.

"Halab's beloved Queen takes good care of the poor here."

"The Queen?" the girls asked in unison.

"Yes, Queen Dayfa Khatun is the current regent ruler, since her grandson is too young to take the throne right now. She is the widow of Az-Zahir Ghazi ibn Salah ad-Din."

Iman's jaw dropped. "Wait. She's the daughter-in-law of Salah ad-Din Ayyubi? The man who conquered Jerusalem?" she questioned with wide eyes.

Abu Yahya laughed as if he had heard a funny joke. "I see his legacy has reached far and wide."

"Do you think we could meet her?" Sara asked with hope.

"I thought you wanted to find your travel companions," he said skeptically. "Now you want to meet Her Highness?"

"Maybe she can help us locate them," Iman quickly replied. "I'm sure she has the manpower."

The old man remained in silence for some time. "I will tell you where to find her at this hour, but you are on your own from here on," he told them.

Sara leaned into Iman's ear. "You think we should agree?" she whispered to her.

Iman nodded. "Allah's with us, remember?" she replied.

"Okay, where is she?" Sara then questioned Abu Yahya.

"You will find her at the women's convent called Ar-Ribaat an-Naasiri. It's a few minutes up this curved road."

While holding on to Iman, Sara leaned sideways and reached out to hand Abu Yahya her water canteen.

"May you be granted the drink of *Al-Kawther*," he prayed for her.

Sara and Iman thanked Abu Yahya and bid him farewell. The road up to the convent was crowded and narrow.

"Maybe we should just walk with Spirit instead," Sara suggested.

Each of the girls dismounted and walked on opposite sides of the horse, carefully making their way through the busy street.

"What do you think she's going to be like?" Iman asked peeking at Sara over Spirit's back.

"The Queen? Gosh, I don't know. I have so many questions I want to ask her. I won't even know where to begin." Sara was smiling ear to ear.

"I hope she has the artifact we need," added Iman.

"Sensei said 'flags of faith.' Does that mean

there's more than one artifact?"

"We'll find out," replied Iman.

"Can you look her up in your *Book of Knowledge*?" asked Sara.

"Okay, hold on."

As Sara held on to Spirit, Iman grabbed the book out of her satchel. She quickly found a passage on Queen Dayfa Khatun.

"Queen Dayfa Khatun was a regent who ruled on behalf of her grandson. She reigned from 1237-1244 AD in Aleppo. She was the daughter of the Ayyubid ruler Al-Adil I and the wife of Az-Zahir Ghazi, who was governor of Aleppo and son of the great conqueror Salah ad-Din Ayyubi. She founded many charities to support the work of judges, scholars and scientists and made sure to take care of the poor. She played a major role in the architectural patronage of Aleppo as one of the most prominent patrons in Syrian history focusing on religious and educational institutions like the Firdaws Madrassa and Ar-Ribaat An-Naasiri (also known as Ar-Farafra). She was favored by her people and known for her piety and as a virtuous, devout believer. Queen Dayfa died at the age of 59 and was buried in the citadel in Aleppo."

"Wow! She sounds amazing!" exclaimed Sara.

"She sure does!" said Iman as she stuffed her book back into her leather satchel. "I'm also glad we don't have to worry about the earthquake or any Mongols."

The girls sighed with relief. As they worked their way through the crowd, Iman noticed Spirit change his footing. He slowed down and then resisted to move forward.

"What's he doing?" wondered Sara as she yanked him forward, but he did not budge.

Iman positioned herself in front of the horse's face and watched him closely. "Look at what he's doing with his eyes." Spirit was moving his eyes in opposite directions –one to the front and one to the back. "I read about this in the animal book Master Rider gave me. Spirit must be seeing something we can't."

Iman searched the crowd behind them. She saw nothing that seemed suspicious or out-of-the-ordinary in the hectic road below. "I don't see what could be wrong," she told Sara, who was also looking around for anything out of place.

Iman watched Sara walk back a few steps and then trip over something hard placed against a brick wall. Sara tumbled clumsily and landed hard on her knees.

"*Bismillah*!" shouted Iman. She ran over to help Sara get back on her feet. "Are you okay?"

Covered in dust, Sara slowly stood up. She displayed her palms which were dirty and scarred in red. She then wiped the knees of her pants with the back of her hands.

"Ouch, that hurt. I didn't even see this bundle," she said pointing to a small hump hidden below a thick potato sack cloth.

Just then, the cloth began to move and a face peered out from underneath it.

"Watch it!" a coarse voice scolded them.

Spirit nickered loudly nearby. Iman realized why he stopped here.

Sara crouched down to apologize to the old woman. She looked gravely frail and weak. "I am so sorry. I didn't see you there," said Sara sincerely. "Is there anything I can do to help you?"

"Go away! Leave me alone!" The woman's teeth were brown and loose like her skin. She rolled over to her other side, facing her back towards Sara. She then hid herself under her make-shift blanket again.

Sara looked up at Iman with big eyes full of shock. She mouthed "whoa!" to Iman silently.

Iman bent down and lightly pressed the lady's legs. "Sister, we'd like to help you. Do you need anything?"

The woman abruptly turned back and glared at the girls. "You don't care about me just like everyone else." The words spit out of her mouth. Her eyes were beady and cold.

"That's not true," Sara said. "We hear the Queen takes care of her people. We are on our way to see her. Would you like to join us?"

The old lady chuckled with disbelief. "The Queen? Ha! Why would she want to see me? I'm a nobody. And you both are fools for thinking she will meet with little girls."

"You won't know until you try," Sara spoke matter-a-fact. "Allah has always helped us find a way as long as we turn to Him."

The expression on the elderly woman's face immediately softened as tears made a wet trail down her wrinkled cheeks. "I've been praying to God for His help."

"Our horse sensed your presence," Iman told her. She took out some dates from her satchel and handed them to the weak woman. "Your prayers are not unheard. Please. Come with us."

Iman helped the woman slowly sit up and enjoy the dates. She then got her to stand on her bare feet. Her legs were shaky under a grimy robe full of patches. She pushed strands of silver, curly hair back into the sides of her frayed head-covering.

The girls worked together to lift her carefully onto Spirit's back.

"I used to be a skilled horsewoman in my day," the lady told Sara and Iman proudly as they walked beside her and Spirit. "There was no rider I couldn't out race or a horse I couldn't tame," she recalled with a snicker.

The Jewels listened with impressiveness.

"Have you lived here all your life?" Sara asked looking up at her, while carefully working her way through the crowd.

The woman waited a few moments before she spoke. "No," she answered softly. "I'm from Antioch."

"Is that far from here?" questioned Iman.

"It's about a day's walk or more."

"What brings you here?" asked Sara.

"The citizens of my city have not agreed with its leadership for many years now. Antioch has been plagued with warfare, earthquakes and economic struggles. I came here in hopes of a new beginning but have not been able to get settled," the woman's voice trailed off sadly.

As pedestrians walked past, they welcomed the Jewels with warm smiles.

"You didn't tell us your name," Iman realized.

"Mary."

Iman and Sara stared at the woman. She was not a Muslim but a Christian.

7

A Challenge

"I thought I was a good Muslim.

I thought I knew a lot of Qur'an.

I thought my prayers were close to perfect.

I thought reflected moonlight was a swan.

And I'm blue so blue.

I'm in a stew – don't know what to do.

My thoughts they brim and brew.

Ya Allah help me truly turn to You.

I thought wrong. I thought wrong."

Hidayah noticed Jaide's eyes well with tears as they read from the songbook. They both listened carefully as the teenage Sensei Elle sat in the middle of a large circled group of girls and sang along with them using the exact same songbook. Jaide then quickly wiped her eyes when Sensei Elle looked up at the Jewels.

"Okay, hand me your songbooks, ladies. Find your usual spots and start revising your lessons. I will come around and test each of you shortly," the young sensei instructed the students.

Jaide quickly put their songbook away in her backpack, so not to confuse theirs with the other students'.

Hidayah stared at the familiar girl that she knew was her sensei but younger. She carefully examined her features and every move as she went around the room. She was so lively and joyful here. It was hard for Hidayah to believe this was the same sensei, who was much more reserved and serious in her adulthood.

"Could that really be her?" Jaide leaned into Hidayah's shoulder and whispered. The great room was buzzing with noise now as students began reciting verses from the *Qur'an* out loud.

You'll find me eventually. Sensei Elle's words echoed in Hidayah's head. "I think she knew we'd go back in time and find her," she whispered in response.

"Hafidha Elle?"

The Jewels turned to the corner of the room where a little girl sat with her hand raised and a *Qur'an* in her lap.

"I'm ready."

They watched as the teenage Sensei Elle made her way to the student and listened to her recite her lesson.

"Whoa. Did you know that Sensei Elle had memorized the *Qu'ran*?"

Hidayah shook her head without a blink.

"Maybe we shouldn't just sit here like zombies," suggested Jaide. "Let's start reading *Qur'an* like all these other girls."

The stillness in Hidayah wore off suddenly. "You're right. Sensei Elle did tell us before we left Vancouver to tie our hearts to the *Qur'an*."

"But what about looking for Iman and Sara or searching for the flags?" wondered Jaide.

"God-willing, I'm sure the *Qur'an* will guide us," answered Hidayah.

Jaide nodded.

The girls then grabbed some copies of the *Qur'an* from a nearby shelf and found open seats on the carpet.

Their voices quickly merged in harmony with the other students. Jaide revised Surah *Yaseen*, a chapter from the *Qur'an* she had memorized recently. Hidayah reviewed the last section of the *Sacred Book*, since she was the most familiar with those closing chapters.

"Don't worry. Hafidha Elle is a really good teacher," a dark-skinned girl softly whispered to them. "She will help you guys get adjusted here in no time."

"Oh, we're not really..." Jaide began to respond. Hidayah quickly placed her hand on Jaide's knee and squeezed it hard.

"Thank you for letting us know," Hidayah interrupted. "We're so glad to be here." She gave Jaide a scolding look to stay quiet.

Jaide pressed her lips together. Hidayah could tell she was embarrassed.

The remainder of the early morning, the Jewels sat amongst the *Qur'an* students and worked on their memorization and recitation skills. It was the most *Qur'an* Hidayah had read in a while.

As the young students headed out for break, Hidayah and Jaide remained behind to help Hafidha Elle tidy up the great room.

"Would you girls like to come with me to pick up some bread and groceries from the market?" she asked the Jewels as they realigned the cushions against the walls of the room.

"Yes, we'd love to," replied Hidayah.

Shortly thereafter, the girls waited patiently outside the home for the young hafidha to join them. The streets were full of villagers now and a symphony of car and bus horns, bike bells, and voices of merchants and pedestrians filled the air.

"I wonder why we came back in time to Sensei's teenage years," said Jaide.

"I think it's nice to see this window into her past," Hidayah stated. "It is surprising, though, how different she is at this age compared to how we know her now. She's much more serious of a person as if she went through some type of hardship before we met her."

"You think we should tell her who we are and let her know how she will be in the future?"

Hidayah's eyes bulged out of their sockets. "No way! That's not our place. Plus, whatever Allah has willed for her, we can't change that. Remember General Hassan back in Turkey? Nothing we did was able to save him."

Jaide quickly lowered her gaze from Hidayah's. Awkwardness hovered over them.

"Yeah, let's not talk about that. It's one of those moments that's still hard for me to think about."

The air was silent between the girls for a few moments despite the hustle and bustle around them.

"Do you think we're going to find Iman and Sara here soon?" Jaide finally spoke up.

Hidayah resisted showing her true feelings to Jaide. Inside, she was afraid they didn't make it on this mission.

"I want to believe they are not far from us, but I really don't know what to think," Hidayah paused here. "Something inside me is saying we should resume this mission as if we are on our own," she was careful and slow releasing these words.

The color left Jaide's face temporarily. "You really think so, huh?"

Hidayah sighed and nodded grimly. She then took out her ancient map from its bamboo case and spread it open in the air. "Okay, so we are here," she pointed to the northern area of Syria. Two small, white flags were pictured over the ninth destination."

"We have to find two flags here?!" Jaide asked, now more worried.

Hidayah examined the image of the flags carefully. "Hmm. I wonder if these are even flags."

"What?! So, not only are the two of us looking for two flag artifacts in this big, foreign city, but we don't even know if we are looking for flags?!" Jaide's voice was getting loud with frustration, and she was breathing heavy now.

The paper crinkled loudly as Hidayah abruptly closed up the map. "Look at your watch. How much time do we have to get back to Vancouver?"

Jaide raised her wrist and glanced at her watch. She then looked up at Hidayah gravely. "Less than an hour and a half," she mumbled. "Of course. Why would we need more time?"

Hidayah grabbed hold of Jaide's shoulders. "Jaide. Stop. Stay with me. I need you to stay positive and truly believe that God will help us through this. You hear me? Now tell me. Why have you been so off as of late?"

Jaide diverted her gaze away from Hidayah and pushed her hands off her shoulders. "I don't know what you're talking about."

"Yes, you do! You weren't confident about your skateboarding, you were hesitant to leave for this mission, and now you are complaining about every little thing. If we are going to make this work, we need to stick together as a team. This is our ninth mission, and we only have a few more left. We need to be stronger than ever. Don't bail on me now, Jaide!" Hidayah's chest lifted up and down as she panted hard.

The sun was peeking over the rooftops of the houses, bringing with it a warm breeze.

"I'm sorry," Jaide's voice had grown softer. "I just haven't been feeling like myself lately. I feel like I haven't been doing anything right, and I feel…I feel…like maybe Allah's mad at me or something."

"We can't think like that, Jaide," said Hidayah. "We need to always keep a good opinion of God and never lose hope in His Mercy. Sensei always tells us of the verse in the *Qur'an* where Allah says He is not Unjust. He won't wrong you, Jaide. Please know that you're such a great friend, and we look up to you and admire your consistent strength. You're always up for a challenge. Don't stop now."

"Really?" Jaide asked, her eyes big with

optimism.

"Yes," Hidayah smiled.

"Thank you, Hidayah. That means a lot to me."

Hidayah hugged Jaide. They stood like that for some time. Then Jaide's eyes fell upon the clean porch step.

"Wow, the mess from the pot is all gone," Jaide stated as she pulled away from Hidayah. "I feel like I should replace the plant I broke."

"Did you bring any money with you?"

Jaide checked her pockets. She pulled out some lint and a piece of chewed up gum balled in its wrapper. She gave Hidayah an empty stare.

"Eww. I don't know how you will be able to buy a replacement plant then."

A strange smirk came over Jaide's face. "I love a challenge."

8

A Piece of the Past

Before Hidayah could challenge Jaide's plan, Hafidha Elle stepped out of the house. It was the first time the girls were able to look at her closely. Hidayah could not help but think how beautiful she looked. The bright morning sun shined against her face. She was glowing in her white *hijab* tucked inside a collared, floral blouse worn over a long navy blue skirt. She had another white scarf loosely draped around her neck and over her shoulders.

"Ready?"

"Yes," the star-struck girls hummed together. They followed the hafidha's fast lead along the cobbled road.

The narrow roads were swarming with people. As they walked past shops and homes, neighbors waved and greeted Hafidha Elle with smiles and salutations. Vendors sold shaved ice, fresh produce, fried goods, and various kinds of sweets, tea leaves and spices. The air smelled of baked breads and desserts, pressed oils, and cheese.

"I'm in Heaven," Jaide said as she licked her lips.

"You both must be so hungry," mentioned Hafidha Elle. "Come with me."

They walked up to a packed outdoor bakery where some men covered in flour quickly pressed and shaped dough into circles. The girls were immediately encompassed in heat, which came from a large oven's open fire. Hidayah and Jaide watched bakers place the circular dough onto a raised iron plate and slide it into a brick oven. Crispy, hot pitas were then pulled out of the oven with long tongs and tossed onto a covered surface. Money and bread flew all around as consumers rushed to grab the fresh bread straight out of the oven. Hafidha Elle grabbed two pieces, handing one to each of the

Jewels. She then took an empty bag and placed a bunch more into it. After, she paid the vendor and turned to walk away.

"Sister, wait!" the man called out.

All three girls looked to see what he wanted. He gave a warm smile to Hidayah and Jaide and handed each of them pieces of taffy. "Welcome!" he greeted them.

"My favorite!" Jaide said eyeing the candy with delight. "Thank you, Sir."

Hafidha Elle then stopped at another shop to grab some fresh cheese. The girls opened their pitas like pockets to let her stuff them. Both the girls' eyes lit up as the cheese quickly melted inside the bread.

"Cool!" said Jaide.

"Good, now eat up. This should hold you over nicely until we get back to the school," said the hafidha.

Hidayah and Jaide exchanged quick glances. They both knew there was no time to go back.

"Oh! Such beautiful children. Praise be to Allah!"

a stout, old lady nearby shouted at the Jewels.

Before they could object, she was grabbing each of them by the face with her course hands and giving them wet kisses on their cheeks. She then placed some chocolates in each of their hands.

"Live long, my children!" she prayed and kept on walking.

Hidayah and Jaide stood frozen as Hafidha Elle quietly laughed with her hand over her mouth.

"You better get used to it," she told them.

As they made their way through the market, more strangers continued to show affection to the Jewels and hand them different sweets.

"I'm running out of room in my pockets for all this candy!" Jaide said in a satisfied manner.

"I just have to grab a few vegetables from the green grocer, and we'll be done," the young sensei informed them.

They approached an open courtyard full of vendors selling different greens on carts. Out of the shadow of the buildings, Hidayah noticed a high hill with a giant stone structure over-looking the city.

"What is that place?"

Hafidha Elle looked up to see where Hidayah was looking. "Oh, that's the Citadel of Aleppo. If you guys are up for it, I would love to take you up there to enjoy some fruit drinks and see the gorgeous view."

"Is it a castle?" Jaide asked as she finished the last of her cheesy pita.

"There's a castle housed within the structure itself, plus a palace, numerous courtyards, military housing, mosques and bathhouses. The citadel was used as a fortress to protect this ancient city. It's been around since the 12th century, maybe even before that. And it's one of the most treasured ancient sights in the world," Hafidha Elle told them proudly.

Jaide's eyes caught the large Syrian flag that waved at the top of the minaret crown of the citadel's mosque. She elbowed Hidayah's side and pointed at it.

"Maybe that's the flag we need to take back as an artifact," she whispered into Hidayah's ear.

Hidayah thought quietly about it. *It can't be*, she thought. The picture on the map shows white flags. Plus, this flag must be fairly recent, not ancient. She shook her head at Jaide, who looked at her in confusion.

"Why not?" she mouthed, but Hidayah quietly dismissed her.

"Could we please go up there?" asked Hidayah. "I would love to see it up close."

"Sure, it's a short bus ride over."

"We can help you carry those," offered Jaide, as Hafidha Elle gathered the bags of grocery on to her wrists. Jaide quickly took hold of a few. She then noticed a boy watering some flowers on a cart nearby. "I'll be right back," she told Hidayah and the young sensei.

"This beautiful, old city reminds me so much of Morocco," Hidayah then turned and said to Hafidha Elle.

"Oh, where have you been?" she asked pleasantly.

"We were in Fes not too long ago."

"That's where the archery academy is!" Hafidha said with delight. "I've only seen pictures of the ancient walled city. I can't wait to see it in person."

"You'll love it. The people there are so hospitable, just like here. It'll feel like home to you, *insha Allah*. Where will you be staying and will you continue teaching *Qur'an*?"

"My cousin lives there, and yes, the *Qur'an* is my life. It has been my shield and my guide throughout my life. My cousin is not only a hafidha, but a scholar of Islamic studies as well. I'll be volunteering part-time at her school while she is on maternity leave. She's expecting twin boys, masha Allah!"

Hidayah's heart began to race as she couldn't believe her ears. *Is she talking about Mus'ab's mom, Umm Amin?* she thought. Before she could ask her what her cousin's name was, Jaide had returned.

"Shall we?" Jaide asked with a goofy expression on her face. Hidayah looked at her suspiciously.

"Yes, let's," and the hafidha led them to a nearby stop, where they boarded a short, white bus almost

91

full to capacity.

The ride to the citadel was brief. Jaide silently showed Hidayah her watch that was flashing only one hour left for them to head home.

Hidayah prayed in her heart for Allah to make it easy for them to retrieve the artifact, to protect Iman and Sara where ever they may be and get them all back home in time. She didn't know what else to do.

The bus dropped them in the middle of a cul-de-sac aligned with beautiful and tall palm trees. A dark-mustache vendor stood nearby with a small cart full of coconuts. Hafidha Elle walked up to him and requested three. He took a large knife, sliced the tops and inserted straws into each.

"Thank you," she said to him, as she handed the girls theirs. She then led them up to a steep, stoned staircase carved into the tall hill above which the grand citadel sat. Jaide and Hidayah's eyes grew big with amazement. They followed the young sensei up to the top, where the view reached for miles and miles. Villagers and cars looked so little from above. The citadel was alive with musicians and performers dressed in traditional garb as well as tourists of all ethnicities.

"It feels like we've gone way back in time, doesn't it?" Jaide softly asked Hidayah, who smiled in agreement.

"This is absolutely stunning," said Hidayah, taking in the surreal view and the height's cool breeze.

The three of them sat on the edge of low surrounding wall. Hafidha Elle shared stories of her childhood and what life in Aleppo was like. The girls listened attentively and felt content to see this side of their sensei. Hidayah especially enjoyed seeing how much the young sensei talked with her hands. She was so expressive and joyful. Once they finished the coconut water, Hafidha Elle gave them a tour of the different gates and sections of the citadel.

"I don't see anything that looks like a flag here," Hidayah whispered to Jaide. "I think we should just head back now."

"Empty-handed?" Jaide asked worriedly.

"I know God will help us. He always has and

will." Hidayah walked up to Hafidha Elle who was a few steps ahead. "I'm sorry, but we must head back now."

"Oh? So soon? But we just started the tour."

"We have a long journey back home and need to leave now," Hidayah's voice was low.

"Where is 'home?'" the young sensei was confused.

"Vancouver, but you will meet us again, God-willing. I'm sure of it." Hidayah and Jaide were standing side-by-side now.

"Who are you?" Hafiza Elle asked –her face inquisitive and serious now.

Hidayah took a few seconds to speak. "We are the Jannah Jewels, and we are trying to help restore peace back on Earth."

"And how can you be so sure we'll meet again?"

"You will find us eventually," Jaide answered. "For now, we must go."

As the three of them made their way back down the large stone staircase, heaviness surrounded them.

Hidayah wished she could tell Sensei more but knew it would not be right to do that. The bus back to the new city was crowded, leaving the girls to stay standing during the ride. They stood quietly, not knowing what to say at this point.

"We know our way back from here," Hidayah told the Hafidha as they stepped off the bus. "Thank you for such a beautiful and unforgettable morning."

"And I almost forgot. Here," said Jaide, handing the bags of grocery back to Sensei. "And this is for you," she pulled out a small flower plant out of one of the bags. "I'm so sorry for breaking the pot this morning."

"Thank you, Jaide. This is beautiful. You didn't have to do this," Hafidha Elle said admiring the plant. "I must give you something in return."

"No, please, it's okay," Jaide objected.

Hafidha Elle slipped her white scarf off her shoulders and handed it to Jaide. "A gift is a gift. It's a *sunnah* and an ancient tradition to accept a gift."

"You're too kind," said Jaide. "May Allah reward you."

The young sensei hugged each of the girls tightly and bid farewell with supplications for a safe journey back for them. Hidayah and Jaide's eyes glistened with small tears.

"I wish Sensei could be as happy now as she was when she was younger," Hidayah said to Jaide as they watched their younger Sensei Elle walk away. "Let's pray that God brings her happiness again."

"*In sha Allah. Ameen,*" Jaide prayed.

"Hey, how'd you afford to buy that flower plant for her anyway?"

Jaide laughed. "I told the little boy who was selling them that I would trade all my candy for it, and he agreed."

Hidayah's jaw dropped. "YOU gave up food for a plant? No way!"

"I told you I love a challenge!" Jaide reminded Hidayah, whipping Sensei's scarf in the air to celebrate. Suddenly, a strong gust of wind flew past from a moving car. Jaide's grip loosened, sending the scarf flying. "Oh no! Sensei's scarf!"

Jaide quickly pulled out her electric skateboard and hopped on, pulling Hidayah on to it behind her. They whizzed after the scarf, weaving their way through cars, walkers and vendor carts.

"I can't catch up to it!" Jaide yelled.

"What do we do?!"

"Hold on!" Jaide commanded Hidayah, who then closed her eyes, grabbed Jaide's waist and held on tightly.

Jaide lowered herself and then lifted upwards. Hidayah suddenly felt light-weight and could tell they were flying in midair. She realized Jaide was successfully doing her Ollie. Hidayah then opened her eyes as they landed smoothly with the board right behind a white delivery truck.

"Grab on to its bumper!" instructed Jaide, turning the board parallel, and bringing Hidayah to her side now. The girls held on to the back of the truck, keeping themselves close to the ground and

out of the driver's sight.

"Woohoo!" shouted Jaide.

Hidayah's knees were shaking, and her eyes were bursting out of her head. She was scared for her life.

"I see the scarf!" Jaide said pointing to the left. It had landed on a girl's head. "On three, slowly let go, and I'll steer us back to it," she told Hidayah. "One. Two. Three!"

The truck kept driving ahead. The girls repositioned themselves with the board and headed over to find the scarf. As they neared the girl on the side of the road, Hidayah noticed her holding the scarf with a neon cast on her arm. She turned back towards the Jewels, who immediately came to a halt when they saw her familiar face. There was no mistaking those steel gray eyes.

"*It's Jasmin.*"

9

A Flag of Faith

The cool breeze smelled of jasmine flowers. Iman and Sara carefully helped Mary dismount Spirit and then tied him to the trunk of a palm tree outside the convent.

As they walked through the entrance of the large building, a sense of calmness came over the Jewels. The convent was topped with oriental motifs and decorated with traditional Islamic calligraphy. They followed a corridor leading to a square-shaped courtyard with a fountain in its center. Women, young and old, dressed in long robes and veils draped over their heads and shoulders walked to and fro. Some carried books in their hands, others baskets with food and various supplies.

"May I help you?" a young woman approached Mary and the Jewels from behind.

"Greetings of Peace," Sara turned and greeted her. "We would like to meet Queen Dayfa Khatun."

"And what business do you have with the queen?"

"This is Ms. Mary, who is a fairly new resident of the queen's city and needs help getting settled here. She traveled here all the way from Antioch," Sara responded.

The woman looked Mary up and down in a concerned manner with her blue eyes. She then turned to Sara and Iman. "What are your names?"

"My name is Sara, and hers is Iman. We would be honored to give our *salaam* to Her Highness."

"The queen has a soft-spot for kids and the poor. You have come to the right place. Follow me," the woman gestured. She led them to a southern part of the courtyard; there was a domed *mihrab* made of marble on an octagonal base and decorated with honey-comb vaulting above it. It was fortified with four large pillars.

They walked into a huge carpeted room full of girls and women sitting in circles on plush rugs. The students were either reading *Qur'an* or listening to teachers give lessons. Sara noticed one teacher, who stood out like no other. She sat near the *mihrab* reciting *Qu'ran* out loud, while students repeated after her. She wore a long purple and gold robe with a hooded cloak of the same colors. Her head was covered in a gold *hijab*, which was veiled under a long purple veil with gold trimming, draped over her shoulders.

"I think that's her," Sara whispered to Iman.

The teacher suddenly looked up at the Jewels. "Continue," she told her students. She gently placed her *Qur'an* on a *rihaal* stand and stood up slowly. She then gracefully walked over.

Sara could not help but think how poised and elegant she was. The Jewels had never met a queen before.

"Peace be upon you," she warmly greeted the Jewels with a soft smile.

"And upon you," they replied in unison.

"Your Highness, I present to you Miss Sara and Miss Iman. They have brought Lady Mary here to you in hopes of helping her get settled in Halab," the female guide introduced them.

"Thank you, Sister Ayesha, for welcoming our guests," Queen Dayfa replied. She then turned to Mary. "Lady Mary, where are you from?"

Mary stood quiet and shy in front of the queen.

Sara took hold of Mary's hand. "Don't be scared. We're here with you," she smiled up at the old woman.

"I come from Antioch, Your Highness. You must be aware of the troubles of our land. I lost all my family and livelihood in the war. I came to your city to seek refuge but have not found my footing. I ask not of you for favors but opportunities to earn my way," spoke Mary.

The small wrinkles around Queen Dayfa's eyes bunched together. She then kindly smiled at Mary.

"We are both creations of the same God," said the queen. "You are of me, and I am of you. He will see no difference between us except for our deeds and our amount of faith in Him. After today, you need not worry as I am here for you. Tell me. What skills do you have?"

A kind of youthfulness fell over Mary's face. She looked alive and was smiling with joy. "Your Highness, I was known as one of the best seamstresses of my village, I was once a horse rider, and I also love to feed people. I can cook for big gatherings."

Queen Dayfa smiled bigger in return. "Well then. It's settled. You will begin working here as of today. We can definitely use someone of your talents here. Ms. Ayesha will show you the west staircase that leads up to our pilgrims' quarters and help you get situated. You may freshen up and find new clothes up there as well. I look forward to tasting your delicious meals."

Tears ran like tracks over Mary's face. She kissed the queen's hand and thanked her repeatedly. She then turned to the Jewels and hugged them both.

"You are my two angels from Heaven. May God continue to use you both to do good. Thank you so much for all your help."

Mary then walked out with Sister Ayesha.

"And I want to thank you too for bringing Lady Mary to my attention," Queen Dayfa said to the Jewels, who simply blushed and lowered their gazes. "So, what can I do for the two of you?"

Sara and Iman exchanged glances at one another, both waiting for the other to speak first.

"Well, if neither of you will speak, then, Miss Sara, I'll ask you to go first."

Sara looked up at the queen. "Your Highness, we have been separated from two of our friends and don't know where to find them."

Queen Dayfa pondered over Sara's words. "And what makes you think they are in my land?"

"We are not sure actually."

"My advice to you would be to go back to where you separated from them. They are probably looking for you both in that same spot," suggested the queen.

"You think so?" asked Sara.

"Yes." Queen Dayfa then turned to Iman. "Now you tell me something I can do for you. You look like a reader to me, and I absolutely love young seekers of knowledge," she said pointing at the two books peeking out of Iman's satchel.

Iman quickly stuffed the books clumsily back into her bag. She then responded, "We are also looking for an ancient artifact."

"Oh? And what's that?"

"It's supposed to be a 'flag of faith'. That's all we know," Iman told her.

Queen Dayfa gestured one of her students to bring over a basket from the *mihrab* area. She then pulled out a white, silk *hijab* from inside it.

"This is our flag of faith. The one who wears it, is a representative of God on Earth just like the two of you," she proudly told them.

Sara and Iman jumped up with delight.

"Thank you so much!" Sara said as Queen Dayfa handed her the *hijab*. She tied the scarf around her neck.

"Is that all?" she then asked the Jewels.

"Actually, there is one more thing," Sara told her.

She then whispered something in Iman's ear, who nodded with a big smile. "We see you encouraging girls to learn *Qur'an* here at your school. We'd like to sing a song in honor of you and your students."

"Oh my Allah, that would be lovely. Please do."

Queen Dayfa and her staff rounded up the students and formed a nice wide circle. Sara and Iman stood in the center with the songbook from Sensei. The room was quiet with anticipation.

The Jewels then began to sing together:

"Page after page,
line after line,
each day I find new wonders in Qur'an.
Page after page,
line after line,
phrase after phrase,
word after word,
each day I find my life enlightened by Qur'an!"

Everyone cheered with joy in the room. Queen Dayfa stood up and walked up to Sara and Iman.

"That was beautiful, girls! Thank you for sharing that with us. We would love for you to stay longer if you can," offered the queen.

Iman squeezed Sara's hand. "You are so kind, Your Highness, but something is telling me we should head back now to find our friends."

"May Allah unite you with those you love," Queen Dayfa prayed.

"*Ameen*," the Jewels hummed simultaneously.

They said good-bye to the teachers and students and made their way out of the convent.

"You really think it's time to go back?" Sara asked Iman as they untied Spirit from the tree trunk.

"Yes, I think the queen was right. We should go back home and look for Hidayah and Jaide at the maple tree," she replied, climbing on top of Spirit.

Sara climbed up right behind her. "Let's go then. God-willing, we'll meet them back home."

The girls rode down the curved road, through the village, past the caravansary and down the open field towards the almond orchard. Sara turned back to look at ancient Aleppo one last time. The Great Citadel was still in sight. It was hard for her to part from what felt like home to her, but she knew she could not stay in the past.

10

Together Again

"Pass the scarf to me, Jasmin, or else," Jaide warned.

"Hidayah. Jaide. Listen to me. We've been looking all over for you," said Jasmin.

Hidayah's heart was racing frantically. She was surprised to see Jasmin after so long. She was alone and unarmed. This was not like her.

"What are you doing here?" Hidayah questioned her. "Where's Jaffar and Mus'ab?"

"We split up to look for you guys."

"You want us to believe that you actually came here with Jaffar and Mus'ab?" Jaide asked cynically. "And now they are conveniently not with you?"

"Yes," she replied.

"Why would Jaffar do that?" asked Hidayah.

"Because…we are trying to find our mother. We believe she is your leader."

"I don't know what is up your sleeve or cast for that matter, but I don't believe a word that you say," Jaide was furious. "Now, hand over the scarf."

Jasmin handed her the scarf without any hesitation.

Hidayah wondered for a second if she was telling the truth after all. She remembered falling for Jasmin's trick back in Spain, where she threw ambergris in their eyes and escaped. She also recalled Jasmin attacking Sara in Turkey and stealing the seventh artifact from her. Hidayah reached to withdraw her bow and arrow.

"That's not necessary," Jasmin said calmly. "I'm not here to hurt you. I just want your help."

Before Hidayah could say more, Jaide pulled her back onto the skateboard. "We don't have time for this sorry act of yours, Jasmin. We're out of here,"

Jaide said as she rapidly skid away.

"Jewels! Wait!"

Hidayah turned back to see Jasmin waving her good arm in the air. She then saw her cover her face with her hands. Hidayah realized Jasmin was crying.

As Jaide and she approached the almond tree, Hidayah felt a tinge of guilt for leaving Jasmin like that.

"You think she was really lying?" she asked Jaide.

"Yes!" Jaide shouted. "She's put us through enough trouble as it is! I'll never trust her!" her breaths were fast and heavy.

"But Jaffar changed. Why can't she? Maybe we should look for Jaffar and Mus'ab and ask them what's the truth. Plus, you have to give Mus'ab his skateboard back."

"Are you serious, Hidayah? I bet they're not even here. If they were here, wouldn't we have seen them by now? Think about all the things Jasmin did to us and what an obstacle she's been on our missions so far. You weren't there with us, but she helped her father keep Sara, Mus'ab and me kidnapped in their house! Now let's go! We lost so much time chasing after the scarf and dealing with Jasmin's nonsense."

Hidayah reluctantly placed her hands on the almond tree trunk.

"Push!" shouted Jaide.

The two Jewels pressed the trunk hard and down, down, down they went sliding through the tunnel. When they reached the bottom, they locked hands and recited in unison, "*Bismillah hir Rahman nir Raheem!*"

*　　　*　　　*　　　*

There was a great whirring sound. Hidayah and Jaide opened their eyes to the warmth of their favorite misty maple tree. The air smelled sweet and welcoming. The lanterns were dimly lit, but they could make out two figures praying nearby.

"Hidayah! Jaide! You're here!" Sara and Iman stood up and ambushed their friends. The four Jewels hugged each other tightly, eyes flowing with tears.

"We were so worried about you two and were praying for your safe return," Sara told them.

"Were you both just waiting here for us the whole time?" Hidayah asked as she wiped her eyes.

"No, we left for the mission just shortly after you guys," informed Iman. "But, we couldn't find you anywhere in ancient Syria."

"You went to ancient Syria?" Jaide said with surprise. "No wonder we never met! We went back to a few decades ago in Syria."

"We have soooo much to tell you guys then," said Hidayah.

"Us too!" shared Sara.

Jaide grabbed Iman's hand. "I'm so glad you guys are okay, *Alhamdullilah*. We need to stick together."

Right then, the Jewels heard footsteps coming towards them through one of the underground tunnels.

"Peace be upon each of you and welcome back," Sensei Elle greeted them.

"Peace be upon you too," the girls replied with relief.

"You four had quite the missions there," Sensei said, emphasizing the plural.

"Yes, Sensei. We all got separated in time," Hidayah responded.

"And yet, Allah brought you all together again safely. That shows the connection that you carry in your hearts for one another. No matter the time or place, your love for Allah keeps you connected. I'm very proud of each of you for not giving up," Sensei beamed.

Hidayah hesitated a bit. "Um, Sensei? We... saw...you."

Sensei's smile grew bigger. "Yes, I saw you too."

"You went on the mission with them, Sensei?" Iman asked confused.

"No, it's complicated," answered Jaide. "That's a story worth sharing over pizza."

"Did you all find the artifacts?" Sensei Elle questioned.

"So, there was more than one!" Sara realized. "We only brought one back, though, Sensei." She untied the scarf from her neck and handed it over.

"And we brought the other," added Jaide.

"Yes, these *hijabs* are our flags of faith," Sensei told them. She then tied a knot between the ends of them. They keep us connected as sisters in Islam and as servants of God."

"I remember seeing that song in the songbook!" Sara gasped.

Sensei nodded and rolled the scarves into the shape of a cinnamon roll. She then handed it to Sara to place into the Golden Clock.

Sara carefully put the scarf roll at the hour of nine o'clock. The walls of the inside of the maple tree glowed from the bright light of the Golden Clock. The two artifacts were accepted and fit perfectly.

"Congratulations, Jannah Jewels. You did a great job," said Sensei Elle.

The girls all hugged and cheered with excitement.

"Sensei, can we please sing the 'Sisters in Islam'

song together to celebrate?" Sara requested.

"Of course."

The girls gathered together with their copies of the songbook and began singing.

"Knowing you has made my days a little nicer.

Having you has made my life a little brighter.

Knowing that you care has made my troubles lighter.

Having sisters in Islam has made my heart feel warmer.

Whoever you are, whoever you are,

whatever your age, whatever your age,

wherever you live, wherever you live...

your smile has won me over.

Your smile has won me over."

As they neared the end of the chorus, they were startled by a loud thud.

"What was that?" asked Hidayah.

A shadow appeared from a corner of the inside of the tree.

"Who is there?" Sensei stood up in front of the girls as if to shield them.

"Mother? Is that you?"

Don't miss the next Jannah Jewels book!

Who followed the Jannah Jewels back to Vancouver? Will the Jannah Jewels be able to find the tenth artifact? What was Jasmin crying about? How will the Jannah Jewels react to this new information?

Find out in the next exciting adventure of the Jannah Jewels: "Intrigue in India."

Find out more about the tenth book by visiting our website at
www.JannahJewels.com

There's A Love

A SONGBOOK

S. Imady

Daybreak Press

Glossary

*Abb: Arabic for 'father'

*Al Kawther: a fountain in Heaven

*As salaamu alaikum: Arabic for 'May God's Peace be upon you'

*Alhamdullilah: Arabic for 'All praise is for God'

*Allah: Arabic for 'God'

*Ameen: same as 'Amen,' it is the Arabic word to close a supplication

*Bismillah: Arabic for 'in the name of God'

*Bismillah hir Rahman nir Raheem: Arabic for 'in the name of God, The Most Gracious, The Most Merciful'

*Hafiza: a female who has memorized the entire Holy Qur'an in Arabic

*Hijab: a headscarf

*In sha Allah: Arabic for 'God-willing'

*Khobz: a type of bread

*Mihrab: a niche in the wall of a mosque toward which the congregation faces to pray

*Qur'an: sacred scripture of Islam

*Rihaal: a stand on to which to place the Qur'an

*Salaam: Arabic for 'peace'

*Sunnah: a practice of Prophet Muhammad, peace and blessings be upon him

*Surah Yaseen: the 36th chapter in the Qur'an

*Wa alaikum as salaam: Arabic for 'and God's Peace be upon you'

To find out more about our other books,

go to:

www.JannahJewels.com

19755143R00080

Printed in Great Britain
by Amazon